CHILDREN'S TRAVEL BOOK SERIES

Eddie the Fox goes to LONDON

YASAR ZANGENBERG

©Pay The Piper Ltd, T/A
Acanexus 2018

ISBN 978-82-92944-16-5

All rights reserved. No part of this publication may be reproduced, stored in a retrieval system, or transmitted in any form, or by any means, electronic, mechanical, recording, photocopying, or otherwise without the express written permission of the author.

Warning: The doing of an unauthorized act in relation to copyright work may result in both a civil claim for damages and criminal prosecution.

Although the author has tried to make the information as accurate as possible at the time of writing, no responsibility for any loss, injury, or inconvenience sustained by anyone using the information can be accepted. The mentioning of companies, individuals, or services in this book does not represent an endorsement; all normal due diligence should be carried out before entering into any contract.

First Edition: September 2018
Author: Yasar Zangenberg
Illustrations: Marina Reshetnikova
Production: Acanexus Publishing
Cover: Carnegie Publishing, Lancaster, UK

To my two beloved daughters
Olivia and Julia

Every day is special if you're Eddie, a fox who can talk and walk on two legs. Today is even more special, because Eddie and his parents are going to London.

Eddie's only problem is deciding which toy to take. He chooses Mister Car. "Don't bring that, Eddie. It was a gift from Granddad! You might lose it," says Mom.

"Oh, don't worry. I won't lose Mister Car," he promises.

The family boards a plane and takes off into the sky.

"Look!" says Daddy. "That is London down there."

From his seat, way up high, Eddie sees it all! There is the river Thames, the parliament buildings, and Big Ben. He can even see the London Eye!

After landing, and unpacking at their hotel, the family visits Buckingham Palace.

"Will we see the Queen?" Eddie asks. "I really want to see the Queen."

"Oh, she is probably very busy," says Mommy.

After watching the changing of the guards, they tour the state rooms.

These are the most splendid rooms Eddie has ever seen. They are so grand that even Mister Car, who is not easily impressed, admits they are wonderful.

The Queen, however, is nowhere to be seen.

Then they head off to the Science Museum. They jump on one of the huge London buses. It's so big it has two floors and a staircase.

From the top floor, Eddie marvels at the hustle and bustle of the big city.

Eddie wants to lift Mister Car up, so that he can see it all too. But where is Mister Car? He was in Eddie's hand not long ago, but now he is gone!

"Don't worry," says Daddy. "I am sure you just left Mister Car in our hotel room."

But Eddie is sure he didn't! His heart races in panic.

They visit the amazing Science Museum. Eddie gasps at rockets, robots, planes, trains, and wonderful complex inventions.

Eddie for a moment forgets all about Mister Car. When he remembers again, he is very sad. "I'm so sorry, Granddad," he thinks in shame.

From the Science Museum, the Fox family strolls to the Natural History Museum, filled with blue whales and dinosaurs, elephants and dodos. There is even a room where they can feel what an earthquake is like!

It is all very exciting! But Eddie wishes that Mister Car was there to experience it.

After the museum they head to the other side of town to see the Tower of London. This is a very old palace for kings and queens, but has also been a prison.

Eddie thinks it is amazingly big. It's almost like an entire town, with towers and houses, inside a castle. One of the buildings contains the crown jewels! Oh, Mister Car would have been so impressed!

Later they head off to Madame Tussauds to see the waxworks.

"Are these real people?" asks Eddie. "They are standing so still!"

"Oh, no! They're not real," Daddy explains. "These are statues made of wax."

They see figures of movie stars and singers, statesmen and royalty. The Queen is there too. The figures look so lifelike, it's hard to believe they are not real.

Eddie wishes that Mister Car was there to see it.

Next they head to the London Eye to see the most fantastic views.

"It is just like the Ferris wheels at our funfairs," Mommy explains, "but much bigger."

Eddie doesn't think it is anything like the Ferris wheels he has seen, because it towers high into the sky!

As the wheel spins, Eddie sees Big Ben, the Tower of London, St Paul's cathedral, and Trafalgar Square. These are the most amazing views Eddie has ever seen. But he wishes Mister Car was there to see them.

"Look!" says Mommy Fox. "That great building is the British Museum. That's where we're going next."

They take a black cab to the museum. Eddie thinks it must be the biggest one in the world! They see Egyptian mummies, the Rosetta Stone, Greek vases, and Roman swords.

Eddie has never seen such wonderful treasures before. If only Mister Car was with him!

Heading back to the hotel, Eddie thinks it could have been the best day of his life, if only he hadn't lost Mister Car! Suddenly he remembers something. He put his toy down in the throne room in Buckingham Palace while he tied his shoelace.

Now Eddie does a silly, naughty and dangerous thing. He sneaks out of the hotel room and into the street. He must get Mister Car, his gift from Granddad!

He jumps on a bus and gets off outside Buckingham Palace. He sneaks past the guards— for being a fast, little fox has advantages— and up the grand staircase.

He opens the door to the throne room, and there is Mister Car, all alone and looking sad.

"Hello, little fox," a voice says. Eddie is startled and turns to see who is speaking.

"I have come for Mister Car," he says. "I have missed him so much."

Then Eddie recognizes the lady, and gives a very good bow.

"Are you Queen Elizabeth, your majesty?" he asks, and the lady says she is.

"It is very nice of you to visit," says the Queen, "and I am glad you found your toy. But it is time for you to return to the hotel. Your parents must be worried!"

Eddie rides with smartly-dressed men in a special car. They see him safely off at his hotel, and Eddie sneaks inside.

"There you are," says Mummy, yawning. "Daddy and I both fell asleep. Where have you been?"

"Oh, just outside," says Eddie.

"I see you found Mister Car," Daddy adds, waking up. "I told you that you left your toy in the hotel."

"Well, this has been a splendid day," says Mommy. "What amazing things we have seen! What was your favourite, Eddie?"

"Seeing the Queen!" says Eddie.

"Oh, yes! But it wasn't the real Queen," says Daddy. "It was only a wax statue."

Eddie grins under his whiskers... Daddy doesn't know that his son has met the Queen of England!

"That will be a wonderful story to tell Granddad," Eddie whispers to Mister Car.

The content of this book is copyright-protected material and must not be copied, reproduced, transferred, distributed, leased, licensed or publicly performed or used in any way except as specifically permitted in writing by the copyright holders, as allowed under the terms and conditions under which it was purchased or as strictly permitted by applicable copyright law. Any unauthorized distribution or use of this text may be a direct infringement of the author's and publisher's rights and those responsible may be liable in law accordingly.

Did you like this book?

Find more similar books on
http://www.acanexus.com/children/

www.ingramcontent.com/pod-product-compliance
Lightning Source LLC
LaVergne TN
LVHW072118070426
835510LV00003B/108